Invisible Threads

**Celebrating the supportive power
of female friendships**

ASHLEY LOGAN

Invisible Threads

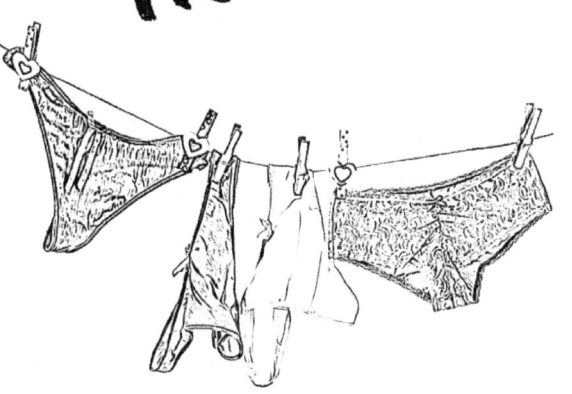

This book is for all my Panties. It's a celebration of you. This book is also for my daughters: Abby, Georgia and CJ—may your drawers be full of the best collection of panties.

Introduction: The Power of Panties

Panties. We all have them, we all wear them. Well, most days.

You're probably wondering if you picked up the wrong book. Why are we talking about underwear? Don't worry, you're in the right place. Panties - in all their shapes and styles - are more than just fabric, they're metaphors for the supportive female friendships that shape our lives.

Each pair in your drawer serves a purpose, just like the women in your life. From the reliable ones you reach for every day to the lacy ones that make you feel bold and unstoppable, panties represent the beautiful variety of roles our female friends play. And just as your underwear collection has evolved over the years, so too has your circle of friends.

This light and quirky book is a celebration of those friendships that have stuck around. *But please, please don't hold onto actual underwear too long - keep your drawer updated.*

This is an exploration of the bonds that elevate us, make us laugh, challenge us, and remind us of our worth. Each chapter will introduce you to a different type of friend—represented by a specific style of panties. We will dive into the strengths, and irreplaceable qualities that make each friend unique. You will probably find yourself nodding and giggling as you read the uncanny descriptions of your favorite panties...I mean friends.

But this isn't just about recognizing your friends. It's also about recognizing yourself too. What kind of Panty Pal are you? How do you show up for the women in your life? Through these pages, I hope you'll gain a deeper appreciation for the power of female friendship and maybe even discover a new way to nurture the connections that mean the most to you.

So, grab a beverage of your choice (depending on your Panty Pal type, your drink type will differ) settle into your favorite spot (maybe far away from everyone), and let's talk about panties and the inspirational women who make life better, one friendship at a time. If you are too curious to wait to find out your Panty Pal type, jump ahead to the quiz on page 60.

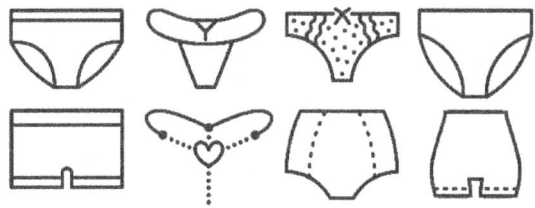

Chapter 1: The Panty Pack

Sometimes, unexpectedly, a Panty Pack is formed. It's what you imagine it to be – a collection of different Panty Pals coming together to form a collective. There is no defined size or prerequisite for this pack. Mine formed out of nowhere…

Here is my Panty Pack origin Story.

It is about a group of women from different parts of Canada who all found each other in Montreal Quebec - and found something far stronger than ever expected. There was no grand vision for what was to come. It just slowly took shape. Organically. And what started as a shared desire for connection turned into something irreplaceable.

We all had kids at the same elementary school, and that was our only link at first. Our friendships were a slow build, like when a snowball gathers momentum rolling downhill. Some of us met through school events, community activities, and volunteering, others were introduced by a mutual friend. Before long, we were all mingling. Shared experiences, brief but meaningful chats at drop-off, and this unshakable feeling that we might just be onto something. The snowball was growing.

It started with pool parties, holiday brunches, and occasional girls' nights out. Each event we spent together felt like a breath of fresh air. That's when we realized it was time to take it further - a weekend getaway to Vermont. No kids. No husbands. Just us. It was the perfect chance to hit pause on life and recharge. We (over)packed and hit the road.

Over copious amounts of wine, deep belly laughter, and many stories, we found ourselves talking about how lucky we were to have found each other. In a world that often feels more divided than ever, here we were, forming this bond. It wasn't about being perfect or having it all figured out. It was about showing up. Every day, for each other.

The name was coined late that night: *we were The Panties.*

Our group chat changed at that moment to reflect our new title.

Our husbands' joint reaction: What? Why? Why The Panties?

It was never really explained…I guess until now.

The best Panty Packs aren't just built on proximity or shared postal codes—they're built on understanding. On people who know when to cheer for you, when to push you, and when to just listen without judgment.

Raising kids can sometimes feel like the loneliest job on Earth for a mother. Even when you're surrounded by people and are lucky enough to have a supportive partner, there are moments when it seems like no one truly understands the depth of what you are going through. You've been told you can "do it all" and "have it all," but what they don't tell you is that you don't have to *do it alone*.

What a relief to read those words, right? I wish someone had told me that 13 years ago when I first ventured into motherhood.

These women—my Panties—have made all the difference. How do they show up? I can't actually list all the ways because this short book would become the length of War and Peace, but I'll list a few. They're the ones who show up at your house for a walk after a message comes through in the group chat that seems 'off'. They're the ones who help you clean up after the dinner party, when they really want to be dancing in the kitchen. They are the ones simultaneously fighting to pick up YOUR kids when you are running late for pickup. They're the ones who listen when you're burned out from work (so are they!) or remind you that you've got this— even when you're convinced you don't. And when you hit that milestone you thought was out of reach? They're there, celebrating like it's their own success, popping champagne on your doorstep. They are the ones mailing you a F.R.I.E.N.D.S mug when your favorite Nonna dies that says, "I'll be there for you", and you know she really is.

When you find your village - when you find your Panties - you'll realize that no matter where you are in life, no matter how chaotic or messy it may get, you are never actually alone.

Every friendship group needs different Panty Profiles. You don't need a whole group of the same type of Panty—you need a variety to support, challenge, and lift you. In the chapters ahead, we'll walk through each *Panty* profile, from the "Supportive Panty" who's always there for a hug, to the "Granny Panty" whose friendship is all about unapologetic comfort and unfiltered joy.

Take a moment to reflect on the friendships in your life.

Which panty does each one embody?

Who is your Supportive Brief, your Adventurous Lace, your Playful Boyshort?

Let this inspire you to cherish and celebrate the women who are there for you and honor the unique ways they make your life richer. After all, every friendship, like every pair of panties, is a little different—and together, they create a beautiful collection.

Now let's discover how each Panty shows up to the panty party. Take note of how many times you find yourself screenshotting or taking a picture of a sentence that captures your friend. Make sure you send it their way.

Chapter 2: The Supportive Brief

Friend Role: The Pillar of Stability
Panty Analogy: The reliable, always-there-for-you brief that holds everything in place.

There are friends, and then there are the *Supportive Briefs*. You know the ones. These are the friends who are there for you no matter what. They don't show up in your life just when it's convenient for them—they show up when it's *inconvenient*, when it's messy, when life is a "beautiful" disaster, and they hold you together like the world's most comfortable pair of panties. It's not always pretty.

The Supportive Brief is the kind of friend who can read between the lines of a text message and knows exactly when you need a phone call, not just a "thumbs up" emoji. They're the ones who remind you to take care of yourself when you're too busy doing everything for everyone else. They'll drop what they're doing to help you with whatever you need, even if that means they're elbow-deep in something of their own. They're your personal emergency response team but with a side of humor, warmth, and empathy.

This is the friend who helps you pick up the pieces when you feel like they've all fallen apart. The one who listens to you vent for an hour and then maybe offers a solution—only if you're ready for it, of course. They give the kind of advice that makes you feel like you can take on the world, but they also know when to just be a shoulder to cry on. And when you feel like you've failed, they're the first ones to remind you that failure isn't final, it's just a pit stop on the way to success.

In a sense, they are the underwear version of duct tape. No matter what mess you're facing, they're going to be the one who wraps you up in a reassuring hug, even if it's metaphorical, and reminds you that you can handle anything—*because you actually can.*

The beauty of a Supportive Brief is that they're reliable. Their friendship doesn't come with the drama of high-maintenance expectations or constant updates. They don't judge you for not having your life together—they're simply there to help you piece it back together when it falls apart. You can count on them to show up when you least expect it, but most need it.

This kind of friend offers a safety net. It's like finding that perfect pair of briefs that fit just right — comfortable, dependable, and ready for whatever life throws your way. There's no question whether they'll be there for you. They *will* be there. Whether you're having a breakdown over a bad hair day or celebrating a long-awaited promotion, they're the first ones to raise a glass to your success (or a cup of coffee if it's Dry January which they legitimately do not judge you for, unlike some other panties we will later discuss.)

In the world of female friendships, this is the type of friend who creates a foundation. They're the ones who have seen you at your worst, and somehow still love you. They don't hold it against you when you're too tired to text back or when you're running late for yet another event. Instead, they make it easy for you to show up as your authentic self, flaws and all.

When Brene Brown talks about vulnerability, she's describing exactly what this type of friendship embodies. Vulnerability is not about oversharing or putting on an emotional display; it's about showing up as your true self — imperfections included and knowing that the person on the other side is going to accept you just as you are. And this is the gift of the Supportive Brief: the ability to be vulnerable without fear of judgment.

So, let's celebrate the Supportive Brief — the friend who is a constant source of stability, the one who always knows what to say (and what *not* to say), and the person who makes you feel like you can face anything, even if you're unsure of how to keep going. When you have this kind of friend in your life, you know you've found something special, something worth holding onto forever.

And as you look around your own circle of friends, ask yourself: who are the Supportive Briefs in your life? Who are the ones you can count on to hold you together when life threatens to tear you apart? These are the friends who make the toughest times feel a little less daunting and the good times better.

In the end, female friendships are a collective force. At the heart of it all, a few well-placed, Supportive Briefs can turn any moment of chaos into something a little more manageable. The power of a true friend lies in their ability to support you through thick and thin, lifting you up when you need it most—and never letting you forget just how strong you are.

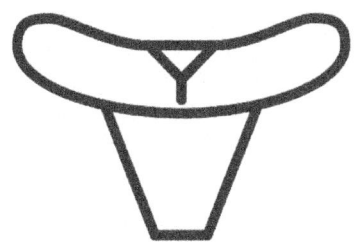

Chapter 3: The Sassy Thong

Friend Role: The Life of the Party
Panty Analogy: The bold, fearless, and unapologetically fun thong that adds spice to your life.

There's a certain kind of friend who lights up every room she walks into. She's confident, she's daring, and she's always ready for a good time. This is the Sassy Thong of your friend group — the one who reminds you that life is meant to be lived boldly, unapologetically, and with a touch of flair.

The Sassy Thong isn't just about fun (though she's mastered the art of it). She's the friend who inspires you to step out of your comfort zone. When you're tempted to play it safe, she's the one saying, "Come on, you'll regret it if you don't." Whether it's dancing like nobody's watching or taking that impromptu weekend girls' trip, she's your partner in crime for all things adventurous and exhilarating.

The beauty of the Sassy Thong is her ability to remind you not to take life too seriously. She has a knack for finding humor in the mundane, turning even the most ordinary day into an unforgettable experience. Spilled coffee on your favorite shirt? She'll laugh it off and say, "Now it's your signature look." With her, every mishap becomes a memory worth cherishing. She is the queen of memes in your group chat, making everyone laugh at relatable moments. And they are often not suitable for most audiences.

She's also fiercely confident—and that confidence is contagious. When you're doubting yourself, she'll give you a pep talk that makes you feel like you can conquer the world. She'll remind you of your power, your beauty, and your worth. "You've got this," she'll say, and you'll believe her because she speaks with the kind of certainty that's hard to argue with.

But don't be fooled into thinking she's all surface and no substance. The Sassy Thong may thrive on fun, but she's also deeply loyal. When you're having a bad day, she'll show up with your favorite things (snacks!) and a list of ways to distract you from the chaos. She knows when you need a pick-me-up and when you need someone to remind you that it's okay to let loose, even when things feel heavy.

The Sassy Thong is the friend who sees the charm in embracing life's imperfections. She'll tell you to wear the bold lipstick, even if it's a little too dark. She'll encourage you to wear that statement dress even if you aren't sure about it. With her, there is nonstop encouragement to be your most vibrant, authentic self.

In a way, the Sassy Thong is a reminder to embrace life with a sense of joy and adventure. She's the friend who teaches you to love harder and live fully. She'll never let you settle for a life that feels dull or uninspired because she sees the potential for magic in every moment. When things are feeling stalled in your relationship, she is there reminding you of what drives you and brings you joy. She isn't trying to steer you in any specific direction, just finding a bold way to recenter you in what matters most.

So, who is the Sassy Thong in your life? Who's the friend that brings out your fun, fearless side? Take a moment to appreciate her. Send her a text, give her a call, or plan your next adventure together. Because if there's one thing the Sassy Thong knows, it's that life is too short not to celebrate every moment - and every friendship to the fullest.

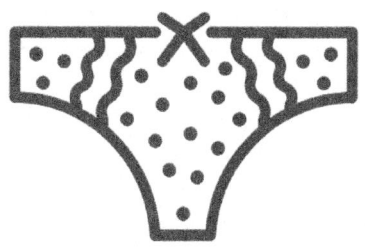

Chapter 4: The Adventurous Lace

Friend Role: The Free Spirit
Panty Analogy: The delicate yet daring lace that inspires you to take risks.

Not every friendship is about stability or comfort. Sometimes, you need someone who shakes things up, someone who pushes you to embrace the unknown and take the leap. Enter the Adventurous Lace. This is the friend who's as bold as the intricate lace of your favorite daring underwear—delicate, beautiful, but unafraid to walk the line of adventure.

The Adventurous Lace is the free spirit of your circle, the one who lives by the mantra, "Why not?" Where others see risk, she sees opportunity. She's the friend who convinces you to try the exotic dish on the menu, play hooky from work to go to the spa with her or say yes to the job that scares you just a little bit. Life with her is a whirlwind of new experiences, and you can't help but feel braver when she's around.

But don't mistake her spontaneity for recklessness. The Adventurous Lace is intentional in her daring. She understands that growth comes from discomfort and that the best stories come from the moments when you're able to step outside your comfort zone. She'll encourage you to take risks not because she wants you to be impulsive, but because she believes in your potential to rise to the occasion. Ok, she also loves seeing you be a little impulsive. She loves seeing a glimpse of your old self shine through the responsibilities of today. She also loves the look on your face before you try something that scares you.

This friend is a dreamer, but she's also a doer. While others might spend hours fantasizing about "someday," she's already making plans. Whether it's enrolling in a class she's always wanted to take or tackling a mountain she's always wanted to climb, she shows you that the difference between a dream and a reality is action.

One of her greatest gifts is her ability to inspire. When you're feeling stuck, she'll share stories of her own adventures—the time she got lost in a foreign city and ended up discovering the best little speakeasy in New York City, or the day she faced her fear of public speaking and ended up nailing the presentation. Her stories don't just entertain; they empower. They remind you that even when things don't go as planned, there's beauty and growth to be found in the journey. She knows that growth is about failing and learning from the failures.

The Adventurous Lace also has a unique way of seeing the world. She'll notice the little things that others overlook—the pattern of the clouds, the rhythm of a busy city, the quiet charm of a forgotten side suburb street. Her perspective reminds you that life is full of wonder if you're willing to slow down and see it. With her, even the simplest moments can feel important.

And when it comes to challenges, she's your ultimate cheerleader. She's the one who'll look at you in the middle of a crisis and say, "You've got this," with so much conviction that you actually believe it. She'll push you to ask for the promotion, start the business, or finally write that book you've been talking about (!). Because to her, you're capable of so much more than you realize.

Of course, the Adventurous Lace isn't without her quirks. She might forget to check in for weeks because she's off exploring somewhere or diving into her next big project or relationship. But when she does reconnect, it's like no time has passed. Her presence is a reminder that friendships don't always have to follow a traditional script. They can ebb and flow like the tides yet remain deeply meaningful.

So, who is the Adventurous Lace in your life? Who's the friend who pushes you to embrace the unknown and reminds you of the magic that happens when you dare to live boldly? Take a moment to thank her for being the spark that ignites your courage. And if you can, take a page from her book and try something new today. Because life's too short to stick to the safe and predictable. Sometimes, you just need a little lace to remind you how beautiful and thrilling it is to take a risk.

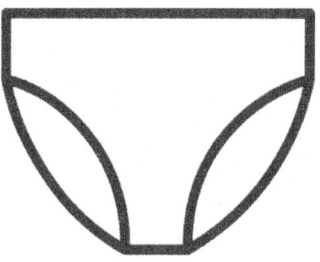

Chapter 5: The Protective Panty

Friend Role: The Guardian
Panty Analogy: The practical, no-nonsense panty
that's there to protect you from life's toughest
flows and blows.

The Protective Panty is the friend who's always looking out for you. She's the one who has your back no matter what, ready to shield you from the world when it feels too harsh. She's all about protection and care—practical, dependable, and unwavering.

This friend isn't flashy, but her impact is undeniable. She's the one who'll step in when things get rough, whether that means offering you a safe space to vent or stepping up to defend you when someone crosses the line. You can picture her face when she hears you've been wronged and even you are scared of this image in your mind. Her loyalty runs deep, and she'll go to great lengths to make sure you're feeling okay. You can remember more than a few instances where she went to bat for you in social situations. She was the type to make sure guys were treating you with respect back in college days.

It is clear that the Protective Panty often takes on the role of the "big sister" in your group. She is probably also a big sister in her own family. She's the one who reminds you to stay grounded, to take care of yourself, and to set boundaries when needed. She'll give you tough love when you need it, but always with your best interests at heart.

Her strength lies in her ability to create a sense of security. When you're with her, you know you're safe. She'll help you navigate life's challenges with wisdom, and she'll never let you face them alone. Whether it's a late-night phone call or a surprise visit when you're feeling down, she's always there to remind you that you're not alone.

The Protective Panty is also the planner of the group. She's the one who makes sure everyone gets home safely after a night out, she was also probably the one who booked the restaurant and hosted the pre-drink., who carries the Band-Aids and snacks on a bike tour in Wine Country, and who always has a backup plan for every single thing the group does. Her foresight and practicality make her an invaluable part of your circle. The weather app is her most frequented app.

But her protective nature goes beyond just physical care. She's also deeply invested in your emotional well-being. She'll check in on you regularly, offering a listening ear and words of encouragement. She'll remind you of your worth when you've forgotten it and help you see the light when you're stuck in the dark.

The Protective Panty is a reminder that strength comes in many forms. She may not be the loudest (sometimes she is)or the most adventurous (her travel bug makes it look like she is, though), but her quiet resilience and unwavering support make her a cornerstone of your life. She's the friend who holds you up when you feel like you're falling, the one who reminds you that you're stronger than you think. She also knows your top strengths and reminds you of them when you can't bring them to the surface.

So, who is the Protective Panty in your life? Who's the friend that makes you feel safe, cared for, and supported? Take a moment to show her your gratitude. Let her know how much her presence means to you. Because in a world that can often feel overwhelming, having a friend like her is a gift beyond measure.

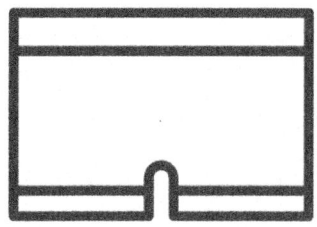

Chapter 6: The Playful Boyshort

Friend Role: The Easygoing Companion
Panty Analogy: The comfortable, versatile boyshort that's perfect for everyday fun.

The Playful Boyshort is the friend who makes life feel lighter. She's the one you can be completely yourself around, free of pretense or pressure. Just like your favorite pair of boyshorts, she's practical, playful, and endlessly reliable.

This friend thrives on simplicity and joy. She's the one who'll join you for a Netflix binge, a walk in the park, a night walk, or a spontaneous coffee date. With her, there's no need for elaborate plans or grand gestures. Her presence alone is enough to turn an ordinary day into something special.

The Playful Boyshort has a knack for finding happiness in the little things. She'll point out the silliest things as you walk by, people watch and create stories of the stranger's lives that you actually believe to be true, laugh at the little things, and remind you that life's best moments are often the simplest. Her easygoing nature makes her a breath of fresh air, a reminder to slow down and savor the present.

This friend is also a master of adaptability. She's the one who'll happily go along with your plans, whether they involve a weekend road trip or an impromptu karaoke night. Her "go with the flow" attitude makes her the perfect companion for any situation. She is your +1 for that work event you are sure your husband won't really want to attend with you. No matter what you're doing, she'll find a way to make it fun. And if you need a person for a duet performance on stage at Karaoke night, you know she will be there for you, regardless of her singing capabilities.

The Playful Boyshort also brings a sense of balance to your life. She reminds you not to take things too seriously and to find humor even in tough moments. When you're stressed, she'll crack a tasteful joke that makes you laugh. When you're feeling overwhelmed, she'll remind you to take a break and just breathe. You go to her because you have experienced this over and over, and love how you feel with her around.

Her friendship is effortless, but it's never shallow. She's deeply attuned to your emotions and knows when you need a pick-me-up. She's one of the first to send a silly meme when you're feeling down or surprise you with your favorite snack just because. Her thoughtfulness is wrapped in playfulness, making her a true gem in your life.

The Playful Boyshort is more than just a friend; she's a lifeline in the chaos of adulthood. She's the one who keeps you grounded while helping you see the world through a lens of lightheartedness. When life gets complicated, she's the simplicity you crave. When everything feels heavy, she's the buoy that keeps you afloat.

So, who is the Playful Boyshort in your life? Who is the friend who has you noticing the beauty in everyday moments—like the way your coffee smells in the morning or the feeling of the way a facemask contorts your face. That's her magic— her gift to you. Take a moment to celebrate her. Send her a text and simply let her know how much she means to you. Friendships like hers are a gift, a reminder that life doesn't always have to be so serious. Channel a little bit of her spirit into your own life. Because the world could always use a bit more of the Playful Boyshort's laughter, kindness, and knack for finding joy in the everyday.

Chapter 7: The Romantic Silk

Friend Role: The Deep Soul Connector
Panty Analogy: The luxurious, silky pair that invites vulnerability and intimacy.

The Romantic Silk is the friend who makes you feel deeply understood. With her, conversations are never just small talk—they're soul talk. She's the one who leans in and asks, "But how are you really?" and then sits with you, fully present, as you unpack your heart. Like the smooth glide of silk against your skin, her friendship is soft, comforting, and yet deeply impactful. And you know her intense eye contact isn't something you can avoid; it's part of the friendship agreement you have.

This friend has a unique ability to create space for vulnerability. She doesn't just listen; she hears you. When you're with her, you feel safe enough to let your walls down, to cry without shame, and to express feelings you've kept hidden from even yourself. She sees past your brave face and gently invites your authentic self to emerge.

The Romantic Silk thrives on connection. She's the one who remembers the little details you share - a childhood memory, your favorite story of a loved one, or a dream you casually mentioned months ago - and brings them up at just the right moment. Her care for you feels like a warm hug, even when she's not physically there.

But her depth doesn't end with her ability to listen. She's also a giver of wisdom. Her advice feels like a whispered truth, gently guiding you toward clarity. When you're wrestling with a tough decision, she doesn't tell you what to do but instead asks the questions that help you uncover your own answers.

This friend values intentionality in every interaction. A coffee date or a late-night chat feels like therapy. She isn't afraid of the hard topics, the raw emotions, or the messy parts of life. In fact, she embraces them because she knows that's where real connection lives.

The Romantic Silk also has a knack for celebrating your essence. She'll write you heartfelt notes, send you songs that remind her of you, or gift you something that perfectly encapsulates your spirit. She is the one who gets you personalized gifts from Etsy, monogrammed just for you. Her gestures aren't about extravagance—they're about thoughtfulness and meaning. She knows that you hate "man-smelling" candles and will get you vanilla scented even though she hates the smell herself.

With her, you feel valued not for what you do but for who you are. She reminds you that it's okay to be vulnerable, to show your scars, and to let people in. Her friendship teaches you that intimacy isn't just for romantic relationships; it's also the glue that binds deep friendships. And when you can't stand being around your boyfriend or partner because they are being 'the worst', she's the one you call up because you know she will get it and fill a quick emotional void.

So, who is the Romantic Silk in your life? Who's the friend that makes you feel seen, heard, and cherished for exactly who you are? Take a moment to honor her. Write her a heartfelt message, schedule an uninterrupted heart-to-heart, or simply thank her for holding space for you. Because friends like her remind us that true connection is one of life's best gifts.

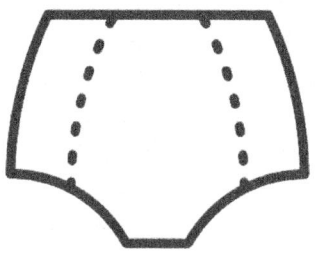

Chapter 8: The Quirky Granny Panty

Friend Role: The Unapologetic Original
Panty Analogy: The funky, comfortable pair that doesn't care about trends.

The Quirky Granny Panty is the friend who reminds you that life is too short to take too seriously. She's the one who wears her mismatched socks with pride, sings loudly and off-key, and makes you laugh until tears stream down your face. Like your favorite quirky, oversized granny panties, her friendship is all about unapologetic comfort and unfiltered joy. She is always the one with the hideous Halloween costume, never the sexy one. The female wrester amongst a sea of playboy bunnies.

This friend marches to the beat of her own drum and invites you to do the same. She doesn't care about fitting in or following the rules. In fact, she revels in breaking them. She'll challenge you to embrace your quirks, wear that bold top you've been too shy to try, or dance in the grocery store - because to her, the only opinion that matters is your own.

Her humor is her superpower. She's the one who'll lighten even the heaviest moments with a perfectly timed joke or an absurd observation. When you're with her, laughter isn't just a possibility—it's a guarantee. Speaking of laughter, she's probably the one who sounds like a dying animal, heaving for oxygen during a laugh attack. Her energy is infectious, and she reminds you to find joy in the most unexpected places.

But don't let her carefree attitude fool you. Beneath her playful exterior lies a deep sense of wisdom. The Quirky Granny Panty sees the world in her own unique way, and her perspective can be surprisingly profound. She'll challenge societal norms, question traditions, and remind you that it's okay—necessary, even—to think differently.

This friend also has a heart as big as her sense of humor. She celebrates your individuality with genuine enthusiasm and never judges your choices. Whether you're confessing an embarrassing secret or sharing a wild dream, she'll be there for you with a kind of unwavering support that feels like she's your personal cheerleader.

Because she is. She might even have some pom poms.

The Quirky Granny Panty also teaches you the value of not taking yourself too seriously. She'll encourage you to embrace your flaws, laugh at your mistakes, and find beauty in your imperfections. With her, you learn that life's messiness is what makes it interesting.

Her friendship is a reminder that you don't have to conform to anyone else's idea of who you should be. She inspires you to be unapologetically yourself, quirks and all. Because if there's one thing she's taught you, it's that authenticity is far more interesting than perfection. In fact, she also reminds you of how fake people's portrayals of their lives are on social media, and urges you to ignore them, or at least look at them through a lens of entertainment. "Don't delete them, you're better than that. Just know that it is a version of themselves they want to project". She's right, and you know it.

So, who is the Quirky Granny Panty in your life? Who's the friend that makes you laugh until your sides hurt and inspires you to be your wonderfully weird self? Take a moment to celebrate her. Share an inside joke, plan a spontaneous adventure, or simply let her know how much her originality means to you. Because friends like her remind us that life is better when you're a little bit quirky.

Chapter 9: The Transformative

Shapewear

Friend Role: The Motivational Mentor
Panty Analogy: The sculpting, confidence-boosting shapewear that helps you rise to your potential.

There's something magical about shapewear, isn't there? It's not just about smoothing out lines or holding things in place—it's about how it makes you feel. A great piece of shapewear doesn't change who you are, but it reminds you of the polished, poised version of yourself that's always been there. It's transformative, not because it makes you someone new, but because it gives you the confidence to fully own who you already are.

That's exactly what the Transformative Shapewear friend does. She's the mentor and the motivator, who sees the best in you even when you can't see it yourself. She's the friend who knows your potential and refuses to let you settle for anything less.

This friend is also the one who challenges you—not in a way that feels critical, but in a way that feels empowering. She believes in you so fiercely that her confidence in your abilities begins to rub off on you. When you're second-guessing yourself, she's there with a pep talk that leaves you ready to take on the world.

The Transformative Shapewear friend pushes you out of your comfort zone, but she does it with care. She's the one who'll suggest you respond to that headhunter who contacted you even though you love your job , sign up for a half-marathon even though you've only run 5km before, or finally launch that side hustle you've been dreaming about. She's the voice that says, "Why not?" when your own inner critic is whispering, "You're not ready."

But her impact isn't just about big, life-changing moments. She's also there for the small, everyday transformations. She's the friend who encourages you to speak up in a meeting, to set boundaries with that overly demanding colleague, or to prioritize self-care without guilt. Her support is like that perfect shapewear—subtle yet powerful, helping you stand a little taller and feel a little stronger in your skin.

This friend doesn't let you settle into complacency. She's constantly nudging you toward growth, but she does it with an understanding of your journey. She knows your accomplishments, your fears, and the obstacles you face. And when the world feels overwhelming—when the mental load of being a wife, a mother, a daughter, a chauffeur, a problem-solver, and a multitasking superhero feels too heavy—she's there to remind you that it's okay to take a breath, to regroup, and to rise again. She feels it too, and isn't afraid to share.

The Transformative Shapewear friend also knows how to celebrate your wins, no matter how big or small. She'll cheer louder than anyone else when you nail a work presentation, master a new skill, or just make it through a tough week. Her joy in your success is genuine and contagious. With her in your corner, you feel like you can tackle anything.

This kind of friendship is precious because it requires a deep understanding of who you are and what you're capable of. It's not always easy to be pushed toward your potential, but with the right friend by your side, it feels less like pressure and more like possibility.

So, who is the Transformative Shapewear in your life? Who's the friend that makes you feel like your best self, even on the days when you're struggling to see it? Take a moment to thank her for believing in you. And if you're lucky enough to have a friend like this, don't let her go—because friends who see your potential and help you rise to it are worth their weight in gold (or in perfectly sculpted shapewear).

Just as shapewear smooths and shapes from the inside out, the Transformative Shapewear friend transforms your life from the inside. She helps you see your strength, embrace your worth, and step into the version of yourself that you've always been capable of becoming.

So go ahead—put her in your friendship drawer, right next to your Supportive Brief and your Sassy Thong. Because a friend like this is not just a luxury; she's a necessity.

Chapter 10: The Past Panty and Future

As I started to write this book, I looked back on my own formative friendships throughout my life. As I thought of the friends I made early on in my neighborhood, at school or through sports and camp, I realized that I was someone who started investing in friendships at a very early age – nurturing friendships was very important to me. Before cell phones, we had home phones, and you better believe I used them regularly to call on friends for playdates. I drew pictures for friends and made them mixed tapes with their favorite songs. I had funny nicknames for everyone. I was a supportive brief and boyshort mixed with quirky granny panty in the making.

I am very much aware of just how special friendships are that can stand the test of time. The ones that grow with you, weather the storms of life, and help you define who you are and what matters most. These are the friendships that don't just witness your life—they shape it. They're the women who knew you when you were dreaming about the future, and who are still beside you as you live it.

I've been lucky to have friends who have walked this long and sometimes windy road with me. These are the friends who remember my curly bangs of the 90s, braces, over-plucked eyebrows, zebra print pants, and who stood by me when I wore a back brace for my Scoliosis in the early years of high school. (Hey, I can see you smirking as you read this…bully). Even though that was a tricky one to navigate, I knew I would have support through it because our friendship was deeper than surface level. They're the ones who text me out of the blue with, "Remember when….?" and suddenly, I'm transported back to those times that somehow don't seem THAT long ago.

These lifelong friendships are a different kind of magic. They're the ones who have seen you at your best and your worst, and they love you anyway. They've evolved as you've evolved, growing deeper and richer with every passing year. Through career changes, marriages, divorces, second marriages, babies, and exhausting phase of endless child-rearing, these friends have been a constant. They've helped me navigate the big questions by reminding me of where I've been and cheering me on toward where I'm going.

Teenage friendships are a unique kind of magic. They're often forged in the intensity of firsts: first crushes, first heartbreaks, first hangover, first big decisions. These friendships are where we learn what it means to be a true friend, to share secrets, to cheer each other on, and to navigate the rollercoaster of growing up.

They are the foundation of what it means to connect - to truly see and be seen.

One of the most beautiful ways these bonds grow is through shared activities. For me, playing AA hockey in Toronto with other girls was transformative. From early-morning practices to grueling tournaments, the rink became our second home. It was where we pushed each other to skate harder, cheered each other on after a well-executed play, and shared conversations in the locker room after tough games. Hockey wasn't just about the sport—it was about forming a comradery. We learned how to rely on one another, communicate under pressure, and celebrate each other's strengths. Those lessons extended far beyond the ice; they became the backbone (crooked, in my case) of how I approach friendships to this day.

Take, for example, the "Sassy Thongs" in our panty profiles—those friends who are bold, fearless, and unapologetically themselves. As a teenager, I often found these friends on my hockey team. They were the ones leading pre-game pep talks, fearlessly taking penalty shots, and owning their presence both on and off the ice. Instead of feeling intimidated, I learned to let their light motivate me to shine brighter. These friendships showed me that celebrating another woman's strength doesn't diminish my own—it amplifies it.

Then there were the "Supportive Briefs"—the steady, dependable friends who were always there to listen and support. Whether it was a quiet conversation on the bench or a reassuring pat on the back after a tough loss, these friendships were my anchor. They reminded me of the beauty in consistency and the importance of showing up for the people who matter.

Not every friendship survives the transition from teenage years to adulthood, but that doesn't lessen their value. Those connections, no matter how brief, taught me how to appreciate different kinds of friends and the roles they play in our lives. They also taught me resilience—how to let go with grace and hold on to the lessons each friendship left behind.

By the end of my teenage years, I understood something profound: friendships, like hockey teams, thrive when everyone is invested in the same goal—connection, support, and growth. These early experiences prepared me for the deeper, more intentional friendships of adulthood—the ones that inspired the panty profiles and continue to shape my life.

So, to the teenage girl who's navigating the complexities of friendship, know this: the bonds you're forming now are teaching you how to connect, support, and celebrate the women in your life. Whether through shared triumphs, quiet moments, or the camaraderie of a team, these friendships are the foundation of the beautiful tapestry of connection you'll weave throughout your life.

Moving onto Camp friends – Friendships under open skies.

There's a special kind of magic that happens at an all-girls summer camp, where the scent of pine mixes with campfire smoke, and the nights are filled with the hum of cicadas. Friendships form in ways that are as enduring as they are transformative. These friendships don't just teach us about connection; they teach us about leadership, life skills, and the strength of a shared journey.

As a tween and teenager, I spent weeks and then later, months of my summers at GBC in Northern Ontario, surrounded by nature and free from the pressures of school and social expectations. From kayaking on glassy Lake Bernard to hiking trails in Temagami that seemed to stretch into forever, we learned to rely on each other, to push past our limits, and to celebrate each other's triumphs. Every shared challenge—from building a fire to navigating a tough trail or completing a 24h solo camping trip on an island nearby—became a lesson in teamwork and resilience.

What made camp friendships so unique was the environment itself. There's something about sitting around a crackling fire, sharing stories, and singing songs under a canopy of stars that strip away pretense. At camp, we weren't trying to impress anyone; we were simply ourselves. Well, less clean versions of our city selves. In that authenticity, we found a connection.

The camp experience taught us how to lead. Whether it was organizing a group activity, mentoring younger campers, or collaborating on a cabin project, we learned the value of stepping up and supporting each other. Those leadership lessons stayed with me long after the summer ended, shaping how I approached challenges in school and now work, where I build leadership programs for others.

The panty profiles come to life at camp in the most apparent ways. The "Playful Boyshorts" were the fearless ones, leading us on daring adventures like midnight swims or improvised talent shows. The "Romantic Silks" were the nurturing friends, always ready with a comforting hug or a whispered word of encouragement during tough moments. And the "Granny Panties" brought joy and levity, ensuring that every challenge was met with laughter and a sense of fun.

These camp friendships didn't end when summer did.

They became the bedrock of who I am today. Even as life pulled us in different directions — college, careers, families — we carried pieces of those GBC summers with us. The lessons we learned under the open skies became guiding principles in our adult lives: how to lean on others, how to lift them up, and how to find joy even in the toughest moments.

The beauty of camp friendships is that they transcend time. Decades later, when I reconnect with my camp friends, it's as if no time has passed. The laughter comes just as easily, the memories flood back, and the bond feels as strong as ever. These relationships remind me of the importance of carving out time for connection, even in the busiest seasons of life. They also remind me of the value of simplicity—of stepping away from the noise of the world to nurture what truly matters.

Camp was also where I learned the art of being present. Without cell phones or social media, we had nothing but the moment in front of us—the rustling of the wind through the trees, the sound of paddles slicing through water, the glow of the firelight on our faces. It taught me how to listen deeply, how to savor simple pleasures, and how to show up for the people in my life with my full self.

Even now, I try to channel that campfire magic into my adult friendships. Sometimes, it's as simple as gathering my closest friends for a backyard fire pit session, complete with storytelling that stretches late into the night. Camp taught me that friendships are nurtured in moments of honesty and vulnerability, and those lessons have shaped how I build relationships in every stage of life.

For anyone reading this, I encourage you to think about your own "campfire friendships." They might not have been formed at an actual camp, but they exist in the people who have seen you at your most unfiltered and still love you for it. Take time to nurture those bonds—because friendships built under open skies, whether literal or metaphorical, are the ones that last a lifetime.

As I reflect on these earlier friendships, I'm struck by how much they've shaped the woman I am today. They've taught me resilience, compassion, and the importance of showing up - not just when it's easy, but when it's hard. They've shown me that true friendship isn't about being perfect; it's about being present.

To the women who've been there through the decades, thank you. You've helped me define what matters most and reminded me, time and time again, of the importance of real connection.

I did some research into the history of friendship – was friendship always part of humanity? I wasn't too shocked to discover that friendship, especially female friendship, has a rich and colorful history that stretches back to the dawn of civilization. Long before Instagram memes or brunch dates, women have formed deep, lasting bonds - often becoming each other's greatest support systems, sounding boards, and secret keepers. And in each era, friendships have had a profound impact on how women shape the world around them.

In ancient Greece, philosopher Aristotle argued that the best friendships were those based on virtue, where friends celebrated each other's personal growth and shared a deep moral connection. Flash forward to the 18th century, and the idea of "female companionship" took a more radical turn, with women in salons like those of Paris and London gathering to challenge societal norms and exchange ideas. The bonds formed in those intellectual spaces weren't just about shared laughter, they were about changing the world together.

As we moved into the modern era, female friendships took on a new urgency. In the 1960s and '70s, as women began fighting for equality and freedom, friendships became not only a source of personal fulfillment but a political statement. Feminist movements flourished because women leaned on each other, lending support, courage, and at times, defiance in the face of inequality.

Today, the tradition of women supporting women continues but it looks a bit different. We may no longer gather around candlelit tables to discuss philosophy or protest in the streets together (well, depends, I might if I feel particularly disruptive!) however the power of a good friend, someone who will back you up no matter what, remains unchanged. In a world where we often feel isolated despite being "connected" online, friendships—especially those among women— have never been more important. Whether it's a late-night phone call after a hard day or a shoulder to cry on when things get tough, these friendships remind us of our resilience, our strength, and our ability to rise together.

Throughout history, women have always known that true friendship isn't just about shared memories - it's about building each other up, facing life's hurdles together, and re-minding each other that we're never truly alone.

Imagine a world where women didn't have their closest friends by their side. It'd be a place that feels a little less vibrant, a little less sup-ported, and a lot less fun. Without the bond of female friendships, the collective energy that women bring to their families, communities, and workplaces would be far less impactful.

Think of all the milestones we experience— first dates, promotions, weddings, the birth of children - and imagine facing those moments without someone outside your own close fam-ily to cheer you on or wipe away a tear when the world feels a little too heavy. The laughter that comes from inside jokes, the comfort of knowing someone has your back without question, and the genuine, no-judgment space to share your most vulnerable moments would be missing.

In the professional world, without female friendships, the networks that elevate women's careers and push for more equality would crumble. Without those key allies, there'd be fewer conversations about closing the pay gap, challenging gender stereotypes, or just supporting each other in our leadership journeys. Without friends to bounce ideas off or offer advice, many women would find themselves without mentors or role models to guide them through the tough moments.

On a deeper level, the collective power of women supporting each other in times of crisis, whether personal or societal, would be diminished without friendships. Feminist movements, women's health advancements, or even simple acts of kindness like helping someone through a tough time would lose their potency. It wouldn't be a good look.

Friendship is an ancient superpower. It's amazing what is possible when women band together.

Chapter 11: Friendships That Anchor

Us in Times of Change

When we encounter big life changes, like the transition into parenthood, we often look to our closest relationships for support and guidance. This support usually comes from those who know us best, like our best friends. But what happens when the person we lean on most isn't physically present? How do we maintain the strength and connection of a friendship when distance separates us?

For me, the answer came during one of the most pivotal transitions of my life: becoming a mother. When I learned that I was pregnant, my first thought was to call my best friend. She had already had her first child four months prior, and I knew her experience and perspective would be invaluable. But there was a big issue–she lived six hours away in Toronto, while I was in Montreal.

At first, the physical distance felt like an obstacle. We had always envisioned going through life's milestones side by side, university, starting our careers, and, eventually, stepping into motherhood together. The idea of raising children in different cities, let alone different provinces, was foreign to me. How would we share these important experiences if we weren't in the same place? She was my Bobbsey twin!

I decided to call her immediately after receiving my news. I needed to hear her voice, to have her words of reassurance and guidance. "I'm pregnant, and I have no idea what I'm doing." I told her.

Her response, though, was simple yet real (she's a Protective Panty, always practical and logical): "There's no 'right' way to do this, and none of us have it figured out. But you know I'm here for you." This isn't a direct quote, but that was the idea.

It was this reassurance that helped me navigate the uncertainty that came with my pregnancy. We traded stories about the ups and downs of new motherhood – her struggles with sleepless nights, and my thoughts about what kind of mother I would be. Ah! We shared advice, laughed about the absurdity of us being responsible parents, and talked through the emotional rollercoaster we both faced. In a sense, the physical distance allowed us to approach the experience from a more reflective perspective. We weren't constantly in the trenches together, but we were there for each other in the moments when we needed it most.

When my first daughter was born, I reached out to tell her within minutes: "She's here," I texted. Her response was to hang up and book a train to Montreal. She was soon there, shoving my husband and me out the door to go on a date - our 1-week-old staying back with her because she insisted it was necessary. She was right, and she was convincing.

I can't help but recognize the resilience of our friendship. The distance between us didn't diminish our bond; it helped us discover new ways to support and empower each other. In times of change, especially when faced with something as transformative as parenthood, the invisible threads of friendship often become more visible and more vital. They offer us the strength to face the unknown and the comfort of knowing that, no matter the miles, we are never truly alone.

This is a lesson that applies not only to parenthood but to any major life change. The key to navigating change, especially when it feels isolating, is recognizing that the support we need is not always bound by geography. True friendships offer us continuity, a safe space for vulnerability, and, most importantly, the reminder that we are capable of adapting to whatever life throws our way.

Chapter 12: Connection in the Cloud – Nurturing Female Friendships in a Remote Workplace

For many women, the workplace has traditionally been a space not just for professional growth but also for connection, camaraderie, and even lifelong friendships. It's been a place of escape, of freeing the confines of the home. But what happens when that space is reduced to a screen? The absence of those spontaneous moments can feel heavy—a weight that's often hard to articulate but undeniably present.

In a remote world, the pathways to those connections feel obstructed, and the effort to bridge the gap can sometimes feel exhausting. The question remains: how do you find meaningful connections when the avenues that once felt natural now feel forced?

The truth is, it's not just about replicating old ways of connecting in a new format. It's about redefining what connection looks like in this new landscape. Maybe it's the warmth of an unexpected message from a coworker who noticed your absence in a meeting. Or the way a heartfelt email can convey care in a way that's deeper than a passing comment in the hallway ever could.

These moments remind us that connection isn't about frequency or proximity; it's about intention.

For women who don't have children or large social networks outside of work, this isolation can feel even more acute. Without the built-in structures that often create opportunities for adult friendships, it can feel like the world has narrowed to the borders of a screen. And yet, there's something beautiful about the resilience of women—the way they find ways to reach out, to check in, to hold space for one another even when circumstances seem to conspire against it.

What does it mean to make friends as an adult, especially in this remote era? It means stepping into vulnerability. It means acknowledging that the loneliness is real and that there's no shame in craving connection. It means daring to send that message, to schedule that virtual coffee chat, to ask, "How are you, really?" even when it feels easier to stay silent.

But it's not all heavy. There's humor in this, too-in the way shared struggles over frozen Zoom screens or the antics of pets during meetings can create unexpected bonds. These moments, as small as they seem, are reminders that even in the digital void, humanity finds a way to shine through and persevere.

As a senior leader in a tech company, I've found myself both challenged and privileged by the responsibility of fostering connections. My role involves building leadership programs and informally coaching others, offering them not only tools for professional growth but also opportunities to connect. I've come to see myself as a connector—someone who bridges gaps, brings people together and creates spaces where individuals feel seen and valued. It's not always easy, especially in a remote setting, but the moments when I witness someone gain confidence, form a new bond, or take a step toward their goals remind me why this work matters. These small victories ripple outward, creating a culture of connection that defies the constraints of distance.

If there's one thing women excel at, it's turning the mundane into something meaningful. A casual exchange of a book or a recipe can evolve into a friendship. A collaborative project can become the foundation of trust and mutual respect. The opportunities are there, not in abundance perhaps, but enough to remind us that connection is still possible, even here, even now.

So, to the woman sitting alone at her desk, wondering if anyone notices the quiet days that stretch into quiet weeks: you're not alone. There are others, just like you, who are longing for connection but unsure of how to start. Be the one to take that first step. Send the message. Share the thought. Open the door. Because on the other side of that small, act might be the friendship you didn't know you needed.

And isn't that the essence of female friendship? The ability to see and be seen, to comfort and be comforted, to create something lasting out of the moments we're given. In this remote world, those connections may look different, but their impact is just as profound.

Chapter 13: Passing the Panty Torch –

Teaching the Power of Friendship to

our Children

Amidst the chaos of life, it is easy to overlook the subtle ways our actions impact those around us, especially our children. They weren't joking when they said, "Kids are always watching.". How many times have you been deep in an adult dialogue only to look over and see a set (or more) eyeballs on you, having taken in 99% of your conversation? It's not always easy to think of a child appropriate lie, or backpedal either…

There's one lesson we may not realize we're imparting every day: the power of true friendship.

Children learn by watching, and how we manage our friendships is no exception. When they see us laughing with girlfriends, comforting a friend through tears, or showing up with unwavering support, they're witnessing a masterclass in connection. These moments, small as they may seem, plant seeds of understanding about the value of building and maintaining relationships.

In a world that often glorifies independence, showing our children how equally important leaning on others can be the lesson they need. It teaches them that strength isn't about doing everything alone—it's about knowing when to rely on your "panty pack" for support.

Think about how powerful it is for a child to see their mother prioritize a girls' night, nurture long-distance friendships with care, or extend kindness to a friend in need. We're modeling vulnerability, empathy, and the joy of celebrating others. These are qualities that children will carry into their own lives, shaping how they build relationships with friends, partners, and colleagues.

Friendship also teaches children resilience. When they see us work through disagreements with a friend, repair a misstep, or navigate life changes together, they learn that relationships aren't always perfect, they are hard work, but they're always worth the effort.

We can tell our children about the importance of friendships, but it's what they see that will resonate most. When they witness us laughing until we cry with our Sassy Thong friend, lean on our Protective Panty Pal in times of need, or embark on an adventure with our Adventurous Lace friend, they're absorbing lessons about love, trust, and community.

They may seem like they're just riding in the back seat looking out the window, but they're listening to your phone calls, and watching your body language.

Passing the torch doesn't mean we have to sit down and explain the value of friendship to our kids. It's in the little moments: inviting a friend over for dinner, calling to check in on someone who's struggling, dropping off soup or baked goods, or sharing stories about the friends who've lifted you up. These acts show our children that friendships are a source of joy, resilience, and balance in a busy world.

As they grow, our children may surprise us by identifying their own "panty pack" in their lives—their playful, supportive, protective, or quirky companions. When that happens, we will know that the legacy of friendship we've modeled has truly taken root.

Speaking of kids growing older, as this happens, and they start finding their own way in the world, there's a bittersweet shift. The constant neediness lessens - no more late-night wakeups, no more frantic school projects - but with that may come a certain emptiness, a feeling of "what now?" That's when the power of female friendships becomes even more profound.

When our children start carving out their own identities, there's a space that opens up in our lives. Instead of filling it with guilt, worry, or wondering if our purposes have shifted, we can fill it with something equally powerful: friendship. Female friendships are the balm for the transition from full-time mothering to reclaiming our own time and energy. These friendships don't just stand as emotional support, they are a celebration of the next chapter. Let's make sure we do just that – carve out the time to celebrate. This is your green light to book a girls' night.

You're welcome.

As our kids become more independent, we see our friends stepping into roles that are essential for our personal growth. And when you feel like you've given all of your emotional energy to your kids, these friends are the people that help fill you back up. And it's these friendships, those women who've grown alongside you, that remind you that your journey isn't over, it's just changing. No matter what stage of life you're in, you've got people who will keep you feeling strong.

I think we will find that as our kids need us less and less (or in different ways, really), our friends are there to help us rediscover the beauty of being needed for who we are - our talents, our wisdom, our genuine identity. When the kids fly the nest, we will likely find that our friendships—our panty packs—become even more of an anchor, giving us the courage to face what's next with confidence and an open mind.

Chapter 14: The Lift – Women

Elevating Women

I've been a long-time champion of other women in the workplace and in life. There's something electric about a room full of women who are committed to elevating each other. It's more than just a feel-good mantra; it's a force of nature. When women elevate other women – and I mean highlighting another woman to make her voice stand out, her idea shine brighter, or congratulating her on something she has executed- something shifts in the air- it's not just about individual ambition or success, but about collective power.

In that room, competition doesn't breed resentment, it breeds inspiration. When one woman succeeds, it's not a threat to anyone else's journey— it's proof that it's possible. The energy is contagious, sparking courage, sparking ideas, sparking the kind of collaboration that can change industries, communities, and lives.

What does real elevation look like? Women aren't just elevating each other by giving high-fives or offering flippant compliments. They're building real, substantive support. It's in the honest advice, the tough love, the guidance given when it's needed most. It's in stepping back to let someone else shine, offering a platform where you could easily take the stage yourself, or using your voice to amplify theirs. It's about actively opening doors, creating opportunities, and never letting anyone feel like they have to do it alone. When people feel alone, they retreat further and divisions are created. We don't need more siloes in this world.

What happens when women elevate other women is amazing. It becomes more than a meeting or an event; it becomes a sort of quiet movement, fueled by the belief that every woman has something invaluable to contribute.

And that's the room I want to be in. And that's the room I want my daughters to be in.

Chapter 15: Panty Presence – Always

Felt, not Always Seen

Be honest – when you started reading this book you were wondering about the connection between panties and friendships, and I get why. Even my own mother looked at me with raised eyebrows when I told her the idea. At first glance, it seems like an odd comparison, but when you really dig into it, the metaphor reveals something beautiful, funny, and deeply true about the relationships that shape our lives. Panties and friendship both serve as essential support systems, giving us comfort, confidence, and a sense of security when we need it most.

Friendships, like panties, come in all shapes, sizes, and styles. Just as every pair of panties in your drawer serves a unique purpose, every friend in your life plays a different role. Together, they create a collection - diverse, colorful, and perfectly suited to all the highs and lows that life throws your way. Each friend adds something special to your story, and like a favorite pair of underwear, their presence is often unseen but always felt.

As women, *we carry so much*. The invisible mental load of being a wife, mother, daughter, friend, professional, coach, chauffeur, line chef, masseuse, nurse, tutor, and more can feel overwhelming at times. We juggle schedules, care for others, and manage the endless stream of to-do lists that come with today's life. It's in the midst of this chaos that our friendships become lifelines. They're the supportive waistband that keeps us steady when we're stretched too thin (every-day, amirite?).

One of the greatest joys in life is finding friends who fit you just right. They're the ones who don't pinch, pull, or restrict, they simply let you be yourself. They celebrate your quirks, pick you up when you're down, and remind you to laugh when life feels overwhelming. They're with you for the wild nights and the quiet days, the triumphs and the heartbreaks, the silly moments and the soul-baring conver-sations. They co-parent with you at the park when the kids are making you both stir crazy in the house. They may even pack snacks for your kids when you forget them. I have one panty pal who is like a wizard – always equipped with multiple snacks in her bag at any moment.

The power of friendship lies in its ability to make us feel seen, heard, and loved. It's in the way a friend's text can brighten your day, or how a shared laugh can turn a bad moment into a great memory. It's in the comfort of knowing someone has your back, no matter what. And it's knowing you are that kind of support for someone else too.

So, as we wrap up this journey, take a moment to reflect on the friendships in your life. Which panty does each one most typically embody? Who is your Supportive Brief, your Adventurous Lace, your Playful Boyshort? Think about the women around you who inspire you to be your best self.

Friendships are the fabric of a life well-lived. They're not always perfect, but they're always worth it. And just like a great pair of panties, they remind us that life's greatest gifts are often the ones closest to us, quietly supporting us every step of the way.

Here's to the power of panties – all my panties - the incredible women by my side who navigate life's endless demands with grace, humor, and strength.

May the bonds you create with your Panty Pack be the comfort you deserve.

Appendix

Which Panty Pal Are You?

Answer the questions below. Each response has a point value. Keep track of your points to find out which panty type best represents your friendship style.

1. When your friend needs help moving, you are most likely to:
a) Show up early with boxes and snacks, ready to assist. (3 points)
b) Crank up the music and make the whole experience a dance party. (5 points)
c) Suggest taking breaks to explore the new neighborhood together. (7 points)
d) Make sure they're lifting safely and staying hydrated. (2 points)
e) Turn it into a fun, light-hearted day with lots of laughs. (4 points)
f) Sit down with them afterward for some heartfelt reminiscing about the old place. (6 points)
g) Bring along something quirky, like a housewarming cactus or a playlist of funky tunes. (8 points)
h) Offer them a pep talk about how great this move will be for their future. (1 point)
Points____

2.   What's your go-to response when your friend calls crying about a tough day?

a) Listen carefully and offer actionable support to help them through it. (3 points)

b) Crack a joke to cheer them up or share something silly to make them laugh. (5 points)

c) Tell them to grab their coat—you're on your way to take them out for a distraction. (7 points)

d) Remind them that they're safe and supported, no matter what. (2 points)

e) Offer a warm hug (virtual or real) and some feel-good energy. (4 points)

f) Ask questions to help them open up and share more about their feelings. (6 points)

g) Send a hilarious meme or share an offbeat story to lighten the mood. (8 points)

h) Motivate them by reminding them of their strengths and resilience. (1 point)

Points___

3. If your friend comes to you with a wild, big dream, what do you do?

a) Help them make a step-by-step plan to bring it to life. (3 points)

b) Get excited with them and throw in some big ideas of your own. (5 points)

c) Say, "Let's celebrate!" and whisk them off on an impromptu adventure. (7 points)

d) Warn them about potential pitfalls while assuring them you'll have their back. (2 points)

e) Celebrate their enthusiasm and remind them to enjoy the journey. (4 points)

f) Dive deep into their emotions, asking how they feel about this big step. (6 points)

g) Encourage them to embrace their unique vision, no matter what others think. (8 points)

h) Push them to take action, offering advice and encouragement along the way. (1 point)

Points___

4.   What's your favorite type of day to spend with a friend?

a) A relaxed day where you get to help them with whatever they need. (3 points)

b) A wild night out or something that gets the adrenaline pumping. (5 points)

c) Something spontaneous, maybe trying a new activity or discovering a new place. (7 points)

d) A cozy hangout where you can protect their peace and make them feel safe. (2 points)

e) A lighthearted day filled with laughter, snacks, and silly moments. (4 points)

f) A deep, hours-long conversation about life, love, and everything in between. (6 points)

g) A creative day of thrifting, crafting, or doing something a little out-of-the-box. (8 points)

h) A goal-setting session where you inspire each other to dream big. (1 point)

Points___

5. When a friend achieves a big milestone, how do you celebrate?

a) Plan something meaningful that shows how much you care. (3 points)

b) Organize a fun celebration to match their excitement. (5 points)

c) Propose a bold way to mark the occasion — skydiving, anyone? (7 points)

d) Make sure they're surrounded by people who love and support them. (2 points)

e) Bring a fun gift and keep the mood light and celebratory. (4 points)

f) Write them a heartfelt letter about how proud you are. (6 points)

g) Surprise them with something personalized that only they would love. (8 points)

h) Use the moment to encourage them to keep striving for even bigger dreams. (1 point)

Points___

Scoring Guide:

Add up the points from all your answers. Here's what your total means:

1–5 points [or mostly h's]: Transformative Shapewear – You're the motivator, helping your friends grow and reach their full potential.

6–10 points [or mostly d's]: Protective Panty – Loyal and steadfast, you always have your friends' backs, no matter what.

11–15 points [or mostly a's]: Supportive Brief – Reliable and nurturing, you're the friend who holds everything together.

16–20 points [or mostly e's]: Playful Boyshort – Lighthearted and fun, you bring joy and ease to every friendship.

21–25 points [or mostly b's]: Sassy Thong – Bold and daring, you add excitement and energy wherever you go.

26–30 points [or mostly f's]: Romantic Silk – Deeply empathetic, you connect with friends on a meaningful, emotional level.

31–35 points [or mostly c's]: Adventurous Lace – Thrill-seeking and curious, you inspire your friends to embrace new experiences.

36–40 points [or mostly g's]: Quirky Granny Panty – Unapologetically original, you remind your friends to embrace their authentic selves.

The Panty Framework for Support:

How to Show Up for Your Friends

This framework uses the panty metaphors to outline keyways to support your friends, highlighting behaviors and the impact you can have in their lives. Each type represents a specific way of showing up, with practical advice for embodying each role.

Remember: just because you now know your default panty pal type, this doesn't mean you can't and shouldn't flex to other types as a friend. You are likely a combination of a few…

1. The Supportive Brief: Pillar of Stability

- **What It Looks Like:** Being a steady presence in times of crisis or change. Listening without judgment, offering practical help, and consistently checking in.
- **Top Behaviors:**
  o Empathy: Understanding what your friend needs emotionally.
  o Reliability: Following through on promises and being dependable.
  o Patience: Supporting them even when the path forward isn't clear.

• **Impact:** Provides comfort and stability, helping friends feel grounded and cared for during uncertain times.

2. The Sassy Thong: Cheerleader of Confidence

• **What It Looks Like:** Bringing positive energy and hyping your friends up. Celebrating their wins loudly and encouraging them to embrace their best selves.

• **Top Behaviors:**

o   Positivity: Radiating encouragement and optimism.

o   Humor: Lightening the mood and finding joy in everyday moments.

o   Advocacy: Championing your friend's dreams and accomplishments.

• **Impact:** Boosts confidence and self-esteem, reminding friends of their worth and potential.

3. The Adventurous Lace: Catalyst for Growth

• **What It Looks Like:** Encouraging your friends to step out of their comfort zones. Inviting them to explore new ideas, adventures, and perspectives.

• **Top Behaviors:**

o   Courage: Pushing yourself and others to take bold steps.

o   Curiosity: Being open to trying new things together.

o   Creativity: Coming up with unique ways to make life more exciting.

• **Impact:** Inspires personal growth, fostering a sense of courage and adaptability in your friends.

4. The Protective Panty: Guardian of Boundaries

• **What It Looks Like:** Advocating for your friend's well-being. Helping them set boundaries, manage their energy, and protect their peace.

• **Top Behaviors:**

o   Assertiveness: Standing up for what's best for your friend.

o   Compassion: Understanding their struggles without being overbearing.

o   Discernment: Recognizing when your friend needs protection or space.

• **Impact:** Helps friends feel safe, respected, and supported, even in challenging situations.

5. The Playful Boyshort: Companion of Everyday Joy

• **What It Looks Like:** Being the go-to friend for fun and lightheartedness. Making ordinary moments special and offering a safe space for laughter.

• **Top Behaviors:**

o   Spontaneity: Being ready to jump into fun activities.

o   Humor: Sharing laughs and finding joy in life's imperfections.

o   Adaptability: Going with the flow and making any situation enjoyable.

- **Impact:** Eases stress and reminds friends to enjoy the small, beautiful moments in life.

6. The Romantic Silk: Deep Soul Connector

- **What It Looks Like:** Having meaningful conversations and holding space for vulnerability. Creating an atmosphere of trust and intimacy in your friendship.
- **Top Behaviors:**

o   Active Listening: Truly hearing what your friend is saying—and what they're not.

o   Vulnerability: Sharing your authentic self to build deeper connections.

o   Emotional Intelligence: Recognizing and validating your friend's feelings.

- **Impact:** Strengthens trust and fosters a sense of being truly seen and valued.

7. The Quirky Granny Panty: Champion of Authenticity

- **What It Looks Like:** Encouraging friends to embrace their quirks and individuality. Challenging societal norms and celebrating imperfection.

- **Top Behaviors:**
  - Authenticity: Being unapologetically yourself, inspiring others to do the same.
  - Humor: Using laughter to diffuse insecurities and challenges.
  - Creativity: Thinking outside the box and embracing unconventional ideas.
- **Impact:** Builds confidence and reminds friends that they're loved just as they are.

8. The Transformative Shapewear: Advocate for Change

- **What It Looks Like:** Pushing your friends toward their highest potential. Offering constructive feedback and supporting them as they work toward transformation.
- **Top Behaviors:**
  - Encouragement: Motivating your friend to grow and evolve.
  - Honesty: Providing gentle yet constructive feedback.
  - Resilience: Being there through setbacks and celebrating progress.
- **Impact:** Creates a sense of empowerment, helping friends become the best version of themselves.

Panty Quotes: Tough Times with Support

Below are some sample (and let's be honest- expected) quotes from your Panty Pals, each representing their unique style in helping you through a tough moment. You come to expect certain responses based on their panty pal type, and you may even notice yourself picking the panty pal who will give you the advice you "need" to hear in the moment.

Am I right? (I see you nodding).

Supportive Brief (Reliable, Comforting, Practical)

What you'll hear:
1. "You're stronger than you think—let's take it one step at a time, together."
2. "Need a little quiet time to recharge? I've got your back; you're not alone in this."
3. "What's one thing I can do today to help you feel a little better?"

Sassy Thong (Bold, Unapologetic, Fierce)

What you'll hear:
1. "Bad day? You've got this. And tomorrow? That's your day."
2. "What's stopping you from flipping the script and turning today into a 'watch out world' moment?"
3. "Let's make a plan to kick this day to the curb. You know you're too good to stay down for long."

Adventurous Lace (Fun, Playful, Always Ready for a New Challenge)

What you'll hear:
1. "I know today's been tough. Let's take a break and explore something new. Refreshing your perspective could be just what you need."
2. "When I feel stuck, I find it helpful to step out of the routine. Wanna try something to shift this energy?"
3. "This may feel like a lot, but it could also an opportunity. What's a small, daring thing we can do today to change the pace?"

Protective Panty (Supportive, No-Nonsense, Always Looking Out for You)

What you'll hear:

1.   "Okay, let's figure this out - what's the next step we need to take to make this better?"

2.   "You don't need to handle this alone. I'm here for whatever you need, whether it's a plan or just a good hug."

3.   "We've got this Don't worry about anything else. I'll stand guard while you take a breather. Let's regroup and attack this together."

Playful Boyshort (Cheerful, Lighthearted, Upbeat)

What you'll hear:

1.   "Let's turn this upside down and grab ice cream and pretend we're on a road trip"

2.   "You're too amazing to stay down for long. Want to grab a [bubble tea/drink/snack] and start plotting your next move?"

3.   "We can turn this day around with some fun. Let's make a list of fun things to do."

Romantic Silk (Thoughtful, Gentle, Heartfelt)

What you'll hear:

1.   "I know it's tough right now, but I believe in you. You've got the power to turn this around with grace."

Top 10 Ways to Celebrate and Strengthen Female Friendships

1. Get Matchy: Nothing says lifelong friendship like permanent ink. Design a tiny matching tattoo that is symbolic, whether it is an inside joke, a favorite phrase, or a simple symbol. If you're not into ink, do matching rings or necklaces. You can take those off at the end of the day...

2. Host a Night of Nostalgia: Celebrate the era when you met by recreating the time period. Dress like your college or high school selves, blast the songs you used to obsess over, and watch the show or movie that defined your friendship. Order the drinks you loved back then, swap old stories, and relive the memories that made you friends in the first place.

3. Screenshot and Share Memories: Scroll through old photos or chat threads, take a screenshot of a great memory, and send it to your friend with a message like, "Remember this?" and make fun of yourselves a bit.

4. Plan a Friendship Day: Choose a city, pick an activity you have never done before, and set out on an adventure together. Try something unexpected like a cooking class, a psychic reading, or a spontaneous road trip.

5. Create a Personalized Playlist: Curate a mix of songs that remind you of your friends. Include anthems from your wildest nights out, cozy tunes for heart-to-hearts over wine, and songs that define your friendship. Send it to them and play it at your next girls' night.

6. Write a 'Just Because' Letter: Handwrite a heartfelt note telling your friend what they mean to you, how they have impacted your life, and why you are grateful for them. Sneak it into their bag or mail it for a surprise.

7. Celebrate Their Wins Like They Won an Oscar: Whether big or small, recognize your friend's achievements in a way that makes them feel like a superstar. Send a text blast, surprise them with cupcakes, or host an awards ceremony with speeches.

8. Plan a "Power Panties" Exchange: After reading through the Panty Profiles, buy each friend a pair of underwear that represents them. Choose something sassy, bold, comfy, or wild and explain why you picked it. This is a personal and surprisingly meaningful way to celebrate each other.

9. Set Up a Standing Monthly or Quarterly Friend Date: Life gets busy, but friendships need nurturing. Make it a tradition, whether it is brunch, a FaceTime call, or wine on the couch in pajamas.

10. Give the Gift of Time Off: Offer to babysit their kids, take care of a household task, or run an errand so they can have a stress-free day to themselves. Whether it is a full weekend of self-care or just a few uninterrupted hours, showing up in a way that truly makes their life easier is one of the most meaningful ways to say, "I've got you."

Female friendships are magic. Make sure to celebrate them in ways as unique and fun as they are.

From the Author

When I first started writing this book, I didn't realize just how perfectly underwear could capture the essence of female friendships. It started as a quirky thought in my mind, amongst many others. But the more I thought about it, the more it made sense. We don't just have one pair of underwear (hopefully), we have a whole drawer full, each serving a different purpose.

Friendships are the same. We don't rely on just one person to fill every role in our lives — our friendships are a collection of personalities, strengths, and uniqueness. And while we appreciate our friends, how often do we truly celebrate them? Outside of birthdays, how often do we pause to recognize just how much they mean to us? That's what this book is: a celebration.

It's not going to change your world or blow your mind, but it will make you want to share your panty profile with the panties in your life. It will make you want to thank them for the role they play. It will make you want to throw this book into a little bag and give it to all the friends you have. When we start to celebrate the women

Printed in Great Britain
by Amazon